A
WORLD OF POWER,
LIES, & DECEPTION

A
WORLD OF POWER,
LIES, & DECEPTION

RUTH COOMBS

authorHOUSE®

AuthorHouse™
1663 Liberty Drive
Bloomington, IN 47403
www.authorhouse.com
Phone: 1-800-839-8640

First published by AuthorHouse   12/02/2011

ISBN: 978-1-4685-2338-6 (sc)
ISBN: 978-1-4685-2339-3 (ebk)

Printed in the United States of America

Any people depicted in stock imagery provided by Thinkstock are models, and such images are being used for illustrative purposes only.
Certain stock imagery © Thinkstock.

This book is printed on acid-free paper.

TABLE OF CONTENTS

INTRODUCTION

There was a time when our country was dry land, hard work and not much to eat. Our idea of life was exactly what it needed to be. We all knew our parts and we did them well. We grew our vegetables and shot our meat. Tradition was a big part of our lives. The children knew their place. Manners and respect for elders did exist. People respected and enjoyed the little pleasures of life. Family meant something back then even if it was a little abusive at times through the generation. Laws were not there to be broken. There were no convenience stores or visa cards. You bought an item only if you had enough cash. Credit was for the higher up. The delicate and moral women of the house were always a curious sight. They comforted their children, fed the family, and always tended to her husband. They worked as a team. At that time, there were hidden treasures to guide them to live life to the fullest. It took a good heart and a strong soul to survive. The idea that you had to work for everything you had showed in the hands of all fathers and mothers. They were proud of the accomplishments because it was tough times. Do you remember the stories of women going 20 miles down the road to help someone who was sick? On the other hand, maybe you have heard that the men got together and built the neighbour a barn. Where are those days? What happened to the people of this world? The Treasures we have not looked at started with our ancestors' ways. They shared tools and skills from our distant family members. What is it that has brought us to this stage in our world? Is it our fault, the people or is it the Government. Yes, we can blame them if that makes us feel good. I have Hidden Treasures that will bring your heart and soul back to where it should be at Peace. In today's world, nothing is safe and neither are the people. Who do you trust your priest, a nun, banker and my point there is no one? We as a society live in fear every day. Money has become the number one thing in life for survival. We have lost our insight into the world and for that; we cannot see the reality of the situation. Have we become so greedy that you walk over people for your own salvation? The Hidden Treasures of life are revealed through the book. Change is upon us and fear is not going to help. Common Sense is one of life's given tools. It helps to make better decisions regarding your life. The most important factor in life I will share with you later. We have in our country today the largest devastation ever witnessed in our generation. Our world is slowly crumbling because we trusted people in different respectable positions and all of them failed us. Now we are scared to open the door for anyone. Totally cut off from society. Splendid job! We can survive this horrible event with the right mindset and strength of an ox you can make it. Our world is about to change and everything you have and everyone you know is going to be tested. It is ugly, worse than what you are already seeing. This book is my way of letting you see what I see and the Tools or Skills that I have given in the book are to help people survive. Those who turn their heads and walk away will not survive. I am not God, I am not anyone, but a child of God who is given the gift to write and it will help. I am not telling people what to do. I am offering a safe haven in a time we all need it. I cannot sit back and do nothing while there are people everywhere in need. In times of trouble, fear, and anguish, I am here to help things be a little easier with the right frame of mind. Take a chance and enjoy the idea of a better tomorrow. Enjoy my book. I want to help as many people as I can to find peace.

CHAPTER ONE

SLOW DOWN

There was a time we stopped to chat with others. Mom stayed home and greeted the children after school. We as parents took the time to make our kids look beautiful. There were rules to live by and you just knew them. Now we have two family incomes and have no time for anyone. My goodness is all that money and all that time away from family good. No! Go back home to your children. All the running you do in a day gets you nowhere. You become tired, angry, and dishevelled. Stop and look at yourself. What is driving you? What is it that makes you want this life so bad? Society has brought to our attention that money is the only way to survive and that is a lie. No one needs a huge house with a mortgage you can barely afford. The fifth wheels for camping and the resorts and all of it is garbage. People are continually perceived by what they own or have. Forget about your heart or your great personality. The clothes you wear, the car you drive, it is despicable. There is only one judge in my world and that would be God. The crimes committed today are far beyond crimes they are bloody war games. Murders, Shootings, Kidnappings and if you look at the case it will have evidence that money was involved. Ask yourself what is important to you down deep in your soul. What is it that makes you, you. What are your gifts and your talents? What makes you blush, what makes you cry? It is time to stop and get to know you better. You have been lost among the jungle called life. Is it okay that people walk all over you? Have you no respect for yourself anymore. We as a nation have lost the idea of how precious human beings are. We treat each other as if we were dogs. Dogs should not be treated badly either. You cannot just throw people away. Stop, take a breath of fresh air, and start realizing who you are as a person. The uniqueness you have that makes you different from others. Learn the parts of your personality that will be able to give yourself and people around you a gift. We are not robots controlled by our society. The only way things will change is when we individually find ourselves again. Someone told us somewhere in our lives that we were not good enough. The pressure we live with everyday to live up to someone else's standards has ended. This is your life it is strictly up to you as to how you live. There are people everywhere with expectations, deadlines, and stress. When expectations are, there you know that failure may lie ahead. The only expectation or overview you need is if you picture yourself standing by yourself and you are naked. Nothing is around you that you purchased in life. How do you feel? The feeling of humbleness, passion, creativity and more is who you are. Now add the garbage around you and you will see more hoarding than you have ever seen. It is as if the world is scared of loosing something. How tragic our future looks. When you are running all the time, you miss friends, family and loved ones. It is not until they lay before you on a deathbed that you even take the time. It had to come to this or your attention would be somewhere else. We all need rules to live by. It is The Ten Commandments. I always loved the idea that stood for the Ten Commandments. I had the opportunity to be aware of such promise through the Catholic religion but I do not believe in religion with a name. I follow as much as I can the Ten Commandments. The world is going so fast it will eventually throw itself into orbit. It is spinning out of control and change stands before us whether we like it or not. All of us can see what is going on and we are helpless to solve the problem. Reason why. We are looking in the wrong direction for solutions that are not there. We have become a nation who needs someone to tell us what to do. We have lost the ability to think for ourselves and in the interim; we have lost who we are. Why is it that we look at a man or woman these days with such disregard for the unique human being they are? Women as I laugh took bras off and called themselves liberated. I am almost embarrassed to be a woman now a day. We fought for all the equal rights and now you even fight amongst each other. There is no race here. With dignity and respect, you can achieve much more. If we slow down, long enough we will be able to see the big picture. People running around like chickens with their heads cut off. You can only lie and cheat for so long and your pot overflows. What we are doing now is not working. The key to any survival is instinct and self-awareness. No one knows you better than you do. Why in the world would you leave your life up to someone else? They have no idea what you want or need. They are a different person with different needs. Let us be honest here everyone is running for the almighty dollar. The idea that we are going to get out of debt is nonsense. We are busting our butts for nothing. To have higher up people make you think you have to give your money to a bank or Government is crap. You are feeding the system and it will not go away. You continue to feed the idea that we as a culture are helpless and that is the farthest thing from the truth. If this thinking continues we as a country will become communist. Have you heard that Canada, Mexico, and United States want to become one country? Did anyone ask the people how they feel about losing our Canadian heritage? Slow down take a look at where you are. What can you do as a human being today to make your life easier, safer, and more peaceful? Change your way of thinking. This is your life, not anyone else so let us work towards implementing things in your life that make you happy. We have a brain, heart and a soul. To find the answers you have to slow down long enough to see. Life is a privilege not something to take for granted. Be all you can be and do not change for anyone. If you are an honest hard working and caring person, whom are you hurting? It is our human right to believe what you want it is freedom of speech. No one person has the right to make you conform to anything. The sad thing is most people that chose to speak out of the bubble have been murdered or shut down. Why. Some of us are sick and tired of the wars, people dying, and the dishonesty. Do not drag us with you it is not the solution to the problem. We owe it to ourselves to start healing from years of control mongers. The only person that tells me how to live is my lord and I. I know what is wrong and what is right. There is no confusion in my life at all. Everyday people are hurting and the stress levels are humongous. Even our children have learnt to run fast and who gives a shit that you hurt. We have labelled and stamped our kids to death. Leave them alone and help them find the innocence they lost. Our children are born with stress. Moms running here dads running here and I am alone all the time. My goodness have you all lost the truth that children are given to you to care for. They are not yours their Gods children and parents have not stepped up to the plate and admitted their part in it. I do all the time I made huge mistakes. Mistakes are something to learn from not something to be judged by. Who gave you the Leadership role in my life? The five minutes it takes to stop and hug your spouse and children every day is about the same amount of time it takes to thank God. You would have nothing if it were not for him. Have you ever thought about that? Faith is a feeling deep down in your soul where no one can see. No one needs to know. It is not their business. It is a feeling of peace, no stress about today or thought of tomorrow. That is the security of life and it is certainty. I had a life growing up no one would believe. In order for me to move on, I had to look inside and realize the days of anyone controlling me ever was over. I needed to make the statement and I did it my way. There is a line in life and no one should ever cross it. When you take integrity and dignity away from any human being for your own motive, you know you are eventually going down. Look at Hitler he was such a coward he shot himself, his dog and his girlfriend and millions of people. **All in the name of control**. After all that, we still have not learnt a thing. We are fighting a war we have no business in and then we go and train the men how to kill. **What a dam proud nation we should be**. Stop and look at your own values and morals quit looking at everyone else for the answer. It is within you to change so that we all can start becoming people who are proud of themselves. What your worth as a human being has nothing to do with what someone else thinks. We all have opinions they make us assume and we all know what that is. We all look like a bunch of ass's truth told. In a way, it is like being told to mind your own business. We have human beings on Television telling everyone how to live their lives. They are wonderful people and contributed well to society. However, when I heard one of them tell one of their guests to shut up that was when the show lost me. Excuse me, When has the private lives of these innocent people ever been admitted as no entry. Alternatively, is it more important that these individuals take all the credit for solving these issues? The credit goes to the guest who has opened their lives to the world. What courage I would never be able to do that. We do not need this garbage on T.V. I guess my biggest question is why the display can this not be done in privacy or do we all have to bring our dirty laundry to the public to be washed. It for me is just a question. Please do not misunderstand me the people they have saved have been wonderful, and the money is awesome. However, for people to go on Television saying I believe in God and live in huge glasshouses and proclaim we need to fix the world. Money is not saving anyone it is a lie all of it. When you help someone in the name of Jesus, you do not tell a soul. You do it because you care not because there is money to be had. Did Jesus go around looking for credit or a pat on the back? Not a chance you do not have to tell the world your problems. Look for the right inspiration it does not come from T.V. or Newspapers or certain religions it comes from **Faith** and **Self-worth**. It absolutely amazes me when you see someone you know and you ask how things are going. It is life's competition to see who is the busiest. Then you have the ultimate question where do you work. Does it really matter enough that I need to tell you everything about my artificial life? Our people have lost the one important thing to us and that is CHOICES. We do not make our own choices and everything has a reaction. Our reaction is Stalemate. We have allowed certain people to label us all in particular groups which is like herding cattle, sheep, and horses just as an example. We have the Handicaps, Bi-Polar, Skitsophrinics, Street People, and Gay People. Give me a bloody break we are HUMAN BEINGS with names and ancestry and heritage. The result of all this labelling and stigmas that are present in our world is traumatic. The running you do every day is because of fear of not being a part of society, which in the long term traumatizes people. The times I have had the feeling of insignificance in the world I would not be able to count on both my hands. I was humiliated, ignored, abused, and literally brainwashed to believe concepts of this world were beyond my capabilities. Hogwash is how I react to this crime. I took three years out of this world and focused just on the results and I was amazed. I started my own group with no funding but my own finances money is nothing. I wrote my first book and now my second. I have no fear, anxiety, paranoia, stress, or confusion. My life is beautiful for the one reason that nothing in my life happens unless I let it happen. I make the choices needed for my life to be the peaceful place it is. Sadly, enough a person realizes they have the one thing back that was taken from them control of their own lives. Stop running around with the idea you do not have time. That is pure nonsense and all it takes is sitting down reading my book and taking a deep breath. You have the right to slow down and you have the human rights to place in your environment and life the things that make life easier. Scary enough that means to sacrifice all this misconception that you need tons of money to be happy. I pay my bills and have a roof over my head with food in the fridge, I could not be happier with me, and the people I choose to have around me. I finally love my life to pieces. I have the peace I never could have imagined and I am supposedly Bi-Polar.

Chapter Two

Whom do you look Up to In This World?

The people I respected the most in my life were Mother Theresa and Joan of Arc. To me they are two examples of love, life, and survival. In their hearts, they stood up and helped humanity stay strong in times of starvation, wars, and crimes throughout the world. They did not stop in what they believed because of anyone's opinion. Joan of Arc was tied to the cross in front of her village because her faith in who she was and what she stood for was not going to change for anyone. They set her on fire and killed her because she would not think the way authorities wanted her to in that time. She led armies into battle and fought without fear. She and mother Theresa died free and at peace knowing, they did something good in this world. We as children of God have been created with uniqueness in all shapes and forms. There is no one person like you. How beautiful is that for us. Now my mother believed in totally taking care of the kids and her husband. Do you see how you have put everyone around you first before yourself? Sounds very familiar these days making sure your boss, mail carrier, neighbour and so on you cannot upset them. Each individual has some part in wither you are successful or not. We used to look up to our parents or grandparents. That is gone because we have lived a life full of lies. We used to be able to trust and look up to our priest. That is gone as well. I never had the opportunity in my life to have anyone to talk too. Therefore, I did the next best thing I talked to God. With my biological parents gone and numerous people as my family, it left me feeling very lonely. I was protected, taken care of and always had a friend. I realized growing up that the special relationship I had and the laws to follow there were no questions I would not be defeated at anything I tried. To live with a perspective that there is only one way for me to be successful within myself I knew I must BELEIVE in myself. There are four major changes in life. When the metamorphosis begins in each cycle, there are choices to make to suit where you are in life. What stage are you at. Are you a teenager or youth going through peer pressure? On the other hand, are you middle aged and dealing with empty nest syndrome. Where ever we are in life is exactly where you are supposed to be. I learnt a long time ago that we have no control over our lives. We all have a life to lead and the people, obstacles, good times, and bad are just part of life. **YOU are the most important person in this world. How** you feel, how you talk, walk and so on and so on is your business. To wake up every day with no stress, pressures, or obligations of any kind except to you is the answer. I did not say disrespect or take authority lightly. Pay attention to you. What makes you laugh, cry, be afraid, and what is your favourite food. To become more aware of yourself opens doors everywhere in life. Too continually, having to explain yourself is exhausting that is why I write now. Unless you have done a crime or treated anyone with disrespect, you owe no one an explanation. We have yoga, exercise, meditation and they call it centering you. Look at yourself in the mirror and just stand there. Who do you see, what do you see, these are the questions you need to ask yourself before it is too late and your life is finished. I would work 14 hours a day and more just to provide for my kids as a single parent. Exhausted at the end of a day. Then I would go to my committee meetings and keep going. I look back and I see how I tried to live a life I was not suited for. Big home, expensive clothes, all the material garbage I worked very hard for everything. Finding solutions for myself gave me proper insight and decision-making. The things that seemed to be so important to everyone floored me. Therefore, when I lost everything I was heartbroken. It made me realize how unimportant this world really is. No person is going to pay my bills and no one cares about my feelings they are to dam busy with their own lives. That was my moment when I realized how important I was to myself. Do you think for one moment your boss cares what your life is like the idea that people around you care enough to help those days are gone. He does not care and the reason is we try to reinforce in our minds that we are good. The job is all he wants out of you and you can and will be replaced by someone new down the road. It is what life is all about. We evaluate ourselves all the time because of what others say to us or about us. Sadly, enough we end up as if we are trained animals accept we are people. There is no one out there that is going to pat you on the back for your efforts accept you. That is the important thing how you feel about what you did or said has to come from inside. It is time to open up inside and start discovering the hidden treasures inside your soul. They are yours and they are private. To be able to look at yourself and be completely honest with yourself helps you to discover your weakness, your compliments in regards to your personality. It took me 49 years to feel the love and attraction I have for Butterflies. I also found out I love the colour pink. The new discoveries are endless and so inspiring for me that I continue to look at myself everyday to see how I can make my life better than it is today. It is my life and I would like all the beauty that I have discovered in my life every day. We have had hero's such as Elvis Presley, Michael Jackson, Muhammad Ali and the list goes on of people that brought joy, entertainment and most of all they gave of themselves so much to the public that they lost who they were just to make society happy. If who I am as a person is not a breath of fresh air and sunshine then I should stay home. The choice to be happy and peaceful comes from being honest enough with yourself to make changes in your life that you control. There is no other person or idle that is going to make you a better person. That job my dear is up to you. Do your inventory and put in what is positive and take out what is ugly and pulling you down. If it is, friends always negative take a hike, if it your animals at home get rid of them, start organizing your life. If you are messy and the mess is always around fix it quit being messy. If your life is so, busy that you cannot take time to clean, water, and help yourself grow. You have missed what life is all about. There is no one you should be judging or looking at except yourself. God made us children of his and God does not make garbage it is time for human beings to start healing within. Make YOU number one in your life that is the first step. The idea that you compare yourselves to others is ridiculous. Everyone in this world thinks acts and behaves differently because we are DIFFERENT. Number 2 is patience and loving with you when learning about yourself. Take the time to be HONEST about yourself. The distractions that are around us daily take our attention away from ourselves. Distractions are a huge issue in today's world. I remember suffering with abdominal pains and stomach pain for two years until I just could not take it anymore. The pain made me feel like I was dying literally. I put myself first, I had to deal with this immediately, and I am happy to report it was a stomach ulcer. Now that you have discovered new things about yourself, let the good times begin. Be very gentle with yourself just as if the good lord would be with you. There are Books, Computers, Doctors, and the whole world has answers everywhere for everything. Nevertheless, the fact is what is out there may not even be considered anything to help you. **Instincts** are the most important personality trait everyone has. That is your core. Does something or someone make you feel uncomfortable for no apparent reason? Have you ever met someone and they give you the creeps. It is our instinct and it keeps us alive. The basic thing in life is to be able to use all senses in your surroundings at all times. Animals have shown us for years, how to survive. Now we as a nation need to build our life skills so we to can have our instinct back. Ask questions and do not be afraid. The reality is the world is no longer a trustful place to be. So make your world safe by protecting yourself. We have people defrauding for money all over the world. Everyone has lost the ability to think straight because of past trauma and the trauma that still exists in our world. Our children have not a clue what to believe anymore because of what is happening every day. We adults of this world are teaching the exact opposite of what they should be. You do not have to be a huge singer, a great actor, or a famous pianist to be great. This is not the truth. We need to back up and start fresh. A new attitude with a completely new outlook on yourself and your future and the success comes from looking at the reality not what is being publicised. With Commercialism and Advertising being the highest focus point in life, we are excessively influenced by what we see, parents have become so distracted by what they think they have to achieve instead of realizing there focus should be on themselves and family. All of us have answers within. Instead of asking, someone else for an answer stop and look inside. You will discover over time and practice that you will begin to live your life and be happy with your new changes. You will find your feelings for yourself will begin to be more positive. You have no one to answer to but yourself. How cool is that. Baby steps we are learning to walk again and you know you can do it this time because your faith is growing in yourself. Get rid of the garbage or barrage of people around you and you will notice your vision is very good. You will see things that you never thought were possible because you have taken the time to slow down and begin to reunite you with yourself. I am one of those people that fell through the cracks. I lived my life from five years old after being adopted running around looking for approval as a person because of the lack of love I received it was horrible. It taught me survival skills and I never lost who I was a person because of it. I had the life skills training and the faith in God to believe in myself. We cannot be fooled by what is going on in our world anymore. No one can continue in a healthy manner it is to dysfunctional. Our kids have nowhere to go so they use computers, texting, and no communication with any rules to follow because mom and dad have to have a big house. There is so much happening today that our generations today are without a doubt suffering from trauma. The trauma now is even worse because the medications and gooroo tactics do not work anymore. The truth is people need healing in society. Not certain people everybody needs help. We are continually being told through every communication in our world, what to do, and how to do it. It is time to stop allowing yourself to be influenced by others opinions, we all have one and you know what that means. I so hate the word MAJORITY. Ninety percent of the majority that wins has bought, traded, or even paid to help win the majority. However, if you do exactly what you want that is who you are congratulations. You have just spoken out and all for your own opinion. Why is it speaking out and saying I have had enough means you are mentally ill, depressed and all the other diagnoses that labels us. I am here to tell you I completely understand this world is a roller coaster. Stop believing everything you hear and see. The answers in your world are within your heart and soul. When you start following that then you will finally start living YOUR LIFE not some else's. How many times do you see the disregard of proper medical attention? We stand or sit in line-ups with broken bones, fingers cut off as an example. I sadly was the one person in that line up that was more than happy to give my spot at the front to the man standing in extreme pain. He and I after six hours finally received the stitches required with no complaints. Yes, I had cut three of my fingers. Again who is to blame or is there someone person to blame. I have met the most intelligent and inspiring people in the world through my group. They are realizing that they can change themselves and the world around them. By simply being themselves and that changes attitudes in society. Where I live, we have the highest suicide rate within our community and area. We have few good examples to look to today and the reason I say that is because behind every door stands a motive. It could be money, who you know, where you think you need to be in society. Whatever happened to Robin Hood, Superman and all those who helped people just to help people? What I have realized through my lifetime is the only hero in my life is God and I. There was no one there when I needed help and believe me I asked everyone I could think of. The idea of parents being a role model today is rare. We have lost faith in our priests and Leaders. The people are speaking loud and clear that democracy is what they want. Everyone is tired of following the orders of how to live. We are not stupid people we are talking, everyone else is talking, and no one is listening. To see the everyday total destruction of a society is scary.

CHAPTER THREE

Focus

This chapter is the heart of life. With so many things going on in our lives, focus has lost itself. To do anything in life to your full ability you have to have focus. I have heard and gone through all the same symptoms as everyone else. Your mind is racing a hundred miles an hour reaction. I feel Confused, full of anxiety, no sleep, problems breathing, and no energy. These are all symptoms that today many people suffer. There is always action-causing reaction in this country. It does not matter what you do someone has an opinion and there is nothing you can do but ignore it. Stop and focus on that ankle that hurts and you never went to a doctor. Ask yourself why you have waited so long. No one is looking after it but you your body. What about focusing on how you react to things. Your body is a unique creation and you have talents and gifts that are unique and loved by everyone. This country is not going to change until people start to focus on the seriousness in today's world. People are dying for no reason except for the fact society lives in fear every day. I have found over the years, and it could be because of my age, that your well-being and your family's well-being now depend on you. If I had not taken the time growing up to focus on getting back to my blood family I would be in terrible shape. My focus was very important because by finding my father and mother it helped me to know in my heart that I was a beautiful person. Then my focus became stronger and I started searching for help for my health. I was diagnosed Bi-Polar, the meds were perfect, and my life was becoming beautiful too. I had for years focused on the horrible things in my life and it was not until I realized the negative affect people and surroundings had on me that I changed. IT IS WHAT YOU PUT INTO LIFE that matters, not what you take out in this life. Focus on the traits you have that can improve even the smallest thing in your life and follow it. This country is not going to change until people start to focus on the seriousness in today's world. People are dying for no reason except for the fact society lives in fear every day. Our tendencies are to focus constantly on what goes on around us. Murders, earthquakes, and all the disasters in this world. The truth is we have no control over the things that surround us. Focusing helps our jobs, family, relationship with the lord and most important allows you to do the best at anything you do personally. With non-distracting focus the energy levels within yourself are not something you need dare question. No interference in a thought process gives human beings the ability to multitask and work with higher than normal intelligence. When I was a child my focus was always on the ugly areas of my life mind you, I was not in a typically normal family. To stay strong as a child I would focus on my mother and father. Reason being they brought love and joy where there was none. Truly, the brain only reacts to what it sees and thinks. Some people uses a form of meditation, praying anything to slow down the mind long enough to gain back the focus. Focusing is very important in relation to who we are as people. Without focus, you can literally become a stumbling, confused individual who cannot make good decisions. The idea that dysfunction, alcoholism, drugs, or mental illness may be a constant focus in our homes or environment is exactly what is so damaging and distracting. How can anyone youth, child, or adult possibly feel good or do positive things for yourself when your attention is on that garbage. The answer you cannot be successful when you are continually carrying others garbage. Let it go it is not your problem. We can listen and even find someone to help others but from there it is up to you. It is like floating in the sea and your partner maybe anxious and he is so terrified he is pulling you down. I would have no hesitation to save my life first you can help the person but until he controls his mind and actions I am not drowning for him. There is a time in everyone's life that you have met a boundary and survival is up to you. While you have this idea that you are changing someone, I am here to tell you quit taking credit for what the individual did. Focusing on what your neighbour drives or how big the home is can only be destructive. You can change no one but yourself. Yes, you will have continued help from many people but your concern is enjoying what you have and enjoying life. Just imagine how wonderful it would be if you actually took time to find out things about yourself, you have never known. Focus is important in everything we do family, job, friends, community events. These are everyday people we deal with and if our focus is not on what we are doing then a hundred percent achievement or success will not be there. We are allowed to dream, we all want things in life. The big question is it a need or a want. Are you sacrificing time with your children or husband and most importantly yourself? The focus for so many years has been based on rich people, leaders and business to tell us how to live and the reason why because we are all scared of loosing things. Fear took the focus away and made us as a society afraid because we have no idea in the country who is making decisions regarding our lives. We took all eyes off people and focus on big business and the small people it did not matter what happen to us. Take the fear away and know in your heart that what you know is right and wrong so start speaking out. If people have a hard time, hearing it is because they are guilty of it. Focus comes from the mind, body, soul. It is with a deep breath and total silence that you can and will discover a new you. You are the most important in the world you are a human being and to demand respect and work towards kindness and community wellness is here and now. We need to start focusing on becoming the majority and put our world where it should be and everyone knows it. Our excuses as a society have run out for me. It is not hard to see the ignorance and disrespect we have in our government. Now we stand today having to choose a man because we do not have a choice and it is the same staff that frauds our country. I drove to see my mother the other day, I was sitting beside her talking and this woman came by, and she was complaining about how hard her job is. She went on and on, I finally asked; if you do not like your job find another one. Why do you not think of beautiful things? Government this and that just kept going. How sad to see such pain and fear. Have we been so cranky for so many years that we live like that, not for me? We have choices you do not make them you live miserable. People will not smile anymore for anyone. We need to focus on bringing back respect for our elders and learn how to shut up and start listening to people. Take the time to give one person a day a compliment and it does not cost a cent. We need to focus telling people what they do right not wrong in life. Our children need more safety measures put in place to protect our children from pedophiles. We need to focus on supporting our Justice System. The number of cases and calls for help are too big and it is now out of control. It is not any one persons fault; human beings do what they can. Focus, focus, focus on cleaning up ourselves first, and our nation after. Do not focus on the ignorance or dysfunction of others. Completely put a deaf ear to anyone who does not like there life. There are groups and agencies all over for help if someone wants to change they will do the work it takes to do so we as a country have to stop being a crutch. Resources are available daily and everyone walks by one everyday all day long. No one person can heal anyone people do it themselves you have to want to. Any person that is told or becomes part of a group because of maybe a criminal offense sometimes that means they are present against their own will. Focus is your own will. What you focus on in and around you will create how you think and feel. Reaction causes reaction. Stop reacting, live your life, and squeeze every ounce of positive that you can stay focused.

CHAPTER FOUR

ONE WITH NATURE

When I was growing up, I could never understand the meaning of one with nature. I was lucky enough to introduce myself to the Native Culture. The unbelievable humbleness and appreciation for the trees, animals, and nature is humbling. These people eat together and share their culture with their children. They hold dear to them the teachings of their elders. Our society used to be like that. Now there is no respect for our elderly and self-respect is completely gone. There was an order we followed and that kept society in its place. There is little regard to parents or Authority. The saddest thing you can blame no one. How can children grow up to be productive citizens with attitudes like that? There are different cultures all over the world and we as a nation expect these people to reform to our ways. The uniqueness of what they stand for and how they pray or live is none of our business. All traditions are to be recognized and gracefully accepted. We are not here to change anyone. Let people live the way they want. To live and pray the way, they want to pray. Who are we to tell them anything? We allow them into the country now let them do what they have to for themselves and their families. Just because it is different does not make them wrong. For centuries, we have destroyed cultures in the name of power. The Jewish people and the

Ukrainian people were slaughtered because of brainwashing. Our past centuries' have taught us something. We are not a communist country and the word freedom is not hard to understand. No one owns the land. It is there for people to live and enjoy life. Why must we be so ignorant to our fellowman? Bullying, suicide, alcohol, drugs. They are all forms of covering the pain and suffering that exists in our country. Kids shooting other children I cannot imagine the pain they are suffering. Mental Illness is trauma; your brain reacts to everything Emotionally, Mentally, and Psychologically. When after 20 or 30 yrs of dysfunction or abuse your brain can only take so much. The brain shuts down it is tired. In order for the brain to repair itself, it is with medications you can slow the brain and body down and the healing process begins. Just trying to live is hard enough now we have cities full of violence and hatred against our own human species. There is no contest here. We are all trying to live by enjoying the fruits of our labour. Not fighting to reach the top whatever that is. We have a hierarchy and the rich and famous live there and we all know who is at the bottom. We all need to find balance with nature and ourselves. Nature talks to us all the time. Do we listen? David Suzuki has shared on television for years what nature is telling us. If no one has noticed, it is angry. We have abused our environment. We have drilled, spilled oil, gas and all other minerals out of the ground. The animals we have to leave alone this is their country to. Everything in life has a job to do while on earth and we humans have taken over and destroyed everything. The air we breathe now is horrible. The fish in the oceans and all sea bearing animals are slowly dying from pollution. Trees and forests have been cut down throughout British Columbia and Northern Alberta. We need oxygen to breath and everything around us needs to breath. We on earth and everything around us needs to breath. Well done people we are slowly but surely choking our own people to death. We have people sick, starving, and dyeing and with all the countries in the world, you could not go down and build new homes and health care to help them. It does not matter who does it. It matters that someone does. All of us are responsible for the destruction and because we are, it is time to clean up and realize the only part of this world you own is you. Mind your own business and start concentrating on fixing our huge mistake. Black or white we as a people need to work together. Quit judging and stop pointing fingers. The trauma we are all experiencing is worldwide and everyone is in shock and panic. Nature is all around us with butterflies, birds, and colourful beauty everywhere. To believe that out of all species we are the greatest. Here is a wakeup call. We are the lowest in the food chain. We are no more important than anyone else is. It is so shocking to me that some humans think I have to answer to them. If the authority that stands before me has respect and individualism then you have my full attention. If you do not have unconditional love and understanding in your program, I do not want it. I work no matter what it is I work for the people. I will do anything to bring a smile or recognition to everyone I meet. My life as a child had no love in it and it was so hard to keep my head above water at times but I did. I had no one telling me how good I was. Sadly enough it affected me immensely and my behaviours were my reaction to behaviours around me. I was a flower ready to bloom and become something special. However, as a symbol, I was not watered and the personal treatment was total neglect. The thing that amazes me now is because of the terrible treatment. It has allowed me to see people with an unconditional light. My knowledge and appreciation for each individual gives needed recognition to all people not certain people. I have no expectations for anyone or myself. I have found a confidence that I have never felt and that is because I am peaceful in my own skin. What is nature to you? Everything in this world exists so we can use what essentials we have to make our world grow. We can feed the whole world. We can build homes for everyone. Stop being greedy and bring to nature what it needs. Necessities' are not available and that is horrible. There is no reason for women and children living on the streets. Women bare children and should be caring for them. Now women have so many traumas and are having babies so young that they are killing their own children. Nature brings to us instincts. Look at animals they have processes within their groups. They know who is there leader is and they keep order. Animals have rules just like nature. They all care for each other and some animals even care for others young. They work together and if one does not follow the rules discipline is used. We could learn a lot just by studying nature. It is time to see the big picture. The universe connects with the sun and moon. Then it connects to the trees and plant life. Connections to all sea life and then at the bottom of the chain are humans. All these things through energy levels contribute to life on earth. Therefore, if anything is off balance then it unbalances the whole creation. That is why we have to quit touching and removing things that do not belong to us it belongs to nature. Balance is the key to the world and to us as human beings. We are a species to and we are not at the top. It is our job as a people to recognize that when you die nothing goes with you. Human beings took authority over everything and now human beings, nature, and animals sit in fear of the future. That is what happens when you think you are superior. We are teaching monkeys to talk English come on they are monkeys and you as a snoopy human think there are answers for us through them. Leave them alone who cares. Why can you not enjoy something from a distance? We have invaded the animal kingdom. We kill for trophies and hides and for human recognition. The bears and other animals have hurt humans because their sick and tired of being bothered in their own space. Admire it and enjoy it do not destroy it. It is not yours, it is ours, and the animals have just as much right to be here as I do. They are dangerous and we know it. Quit trying to make them human friendly it is not their nature. To touch nature is to put off balance all of nature. We all have our own spaces stay there and leave everything and everybody alone. It does not matter what they are doing what matters is that they continue to populate and live the life of a bear. Then we have the disaster in our oceans. Nevertheless, as beautiful as Mother Nature is she heals eventually. After everything this world has been through, she still grows back lush, new, and beautiful until one day again man destroys it.

CHAPTER FIVE

UNCONDITIONAL ACCEPTANCE

The word unconditional is one that is easy to understand mentally, but try putting it in your heart and actions daily. Acceptance speaks for its self. This for me was and still is the hardest trait to have. I work daily with accepting everything and everyone in my life totally with unconditional acceptance. To do that for me is making sure every day I walk with no judgements or opinion regarding anyone. Now to get even to that point I realized that in order for any change to happen to me I would have to change me. There are days I want to rip the world apart. I have accepted that I will never be perfect. However if I want to be unconditionally accepted then I must practice what I preach. The discipline is very difficult. I found as time went on I found that not only was I accepting of others but I became more accepting of myself. Society has taught all of us to pick apart everything and find those negatives. It is like taking a frog in science class and dissecting it. The differences we all have are fabulous. If we took all the ideas from all these people, we would achieve success not only for ourselves but also for everyone. What is it that makes man want to have control or power? It to me is so ludicrous for no one ever wins. All of us are quite capable of thinking for ourselves and making decisions for ourselves because you who ever you are you have no clue that my needs are mine. Personal privacy is very rare these days continued violation towards neighbours, family, and the work place has become an everyday occurrence in life because someone wants you to do things their way. What happened to living free to be who you want to be? I do not remember calling Joe blow to come and tell me I am not living right. I of course will tell Joe blow very kindly but direct to mind your business go preach to someone else. Everyone is different for the purpose of humility and acceptance. All people have something to offer that is why we have such different and great ideas because we are open to all opinions. To grasp the idea of unconditional acceptance you have to start with you no one but you. If you do not like yourself and your negativity and putting yourself down all the time that is what you, see and feel around you. The biggest journey in life is your own personal journey and it takes courage to look at yourself and see what you can do to make you better. Admitting mistakes, and replacing them with new personal affirmations that are more positive. If we look at it in the proper perspective, you will see that everyone seems to be following someone for the right direction as a society. When we are born, we have love, comfort and a mother and father to call our own. As soon as the mother and father start teaching, the child it is only with time that we discover the control. We are sadly a lot like computers. What society expects from us and everyone in the world is nothing more than control. I remember growing up how people of authority took it upon themselves to tell me daily to stop crying, quit feeling sorry for you and the list went on. The idea that anyone has the right to tell me how to feel is hilarious do you honestly believe I am that stupid to think you know anything about me. So how can that be unconditional acceptance? The children are given the freedom to express themselves in their own personal way. When any one person does something that is not acceptable in others eyes the person ends up as the outsider in society. What happened to freedom of speech and the idea that everyone has the freedom to be just who they are? Between science and religion, they tell us they have the answers to how the world even started. I do not want to live my life around other people's beliefs. Amazingly, the one disease that is killing people is cancer and with all the millions of dollars donated, we have no answer to the cure. Just how stupid do you think people are? As a child with adults who were strangers to me because of adoption, I was given no option but to rely on these strangers to trust. The garbage taught to me in my mind was sick and twisted. Why is it that people today with expectations and rules for themselves expect the same of all human beings? No one asked you to expect anything from me. If I was, left alone to discover what was right or wrong for me. I would have become more excepting of myself. It amazes me how some people actually think that society is incapable of thinking for itself. It burns me big time no one has any right to mould anyone to what he or she think is right. Even babies have instincts. It is our job to make sure we are there to help not take over or control. Man seems to think they are the answer to everything in this life and they are not. We all know our way around the world. We know the difference between wrong and right and we are going to make mistakes. Get used to it. It is my and your life do not let anyone control you or your inner self to please someone else. We are not here for that. I know I am here to enjoy the beautiful skies, birds, neighbours and everything in this life. The only problem is everyone tries to involve him or herself in my life. I learnt a polite and kind way of saying mind your business if you are in my life to judge or be a critic then I would walk you to the door. Anyone who has expectations you had better get rid of them. We are always going to be disappointed if we think others are going to do what we expect. Give your head a shake their purpose for being has nothing to do with you. We all are different but society has not caught on yet that they are a bunch of robots. You have to go to church, you have to go to work the rules are endless and ridiculous. When I tell someone I have Bi-Polar, you should watch the expressions. O my god looks and then there are you okay. Alternatively, how do you live? I want to say I live out of a box, but I know that is not polite. However, really I am so secure with who I am I have nothing to hide. I make mistakes like everyone else and I always will. I know if I asked for advice from anyone, it would be just what it is a personal viewpoint. That is why you have to take everything with a grain of salt. Sorry. This society is full of imitation, entertainment, and advertising. These are not human qualities. We are not great people because of the titles we are given. We are not great people because we control the masses. We become great people by becoming a great person. Mother Theresa, which happens to be my greatest mentor never, did anything in her life with a title. She has always said that this world is full of great people but sadly the most humble and understanding people are the poor. She gave everything of herself to make sure the poor and dying people across the world had hope. She made it her goal to offer the poor dignity and respect. I am not saying you have to be Mother Theresa. I am saying we have a choice in this life. Mother Theresa gave to people the true meaning of life Unconditional love and Acceptance. To be judged by circumstance is very humiliating. We have single mothers, mentally handicap, people living on the streets and no one has a clue to their circumstance. Nevertheless, I have witnessed on numerous occasions the degree of humiliation, degrading and unruly glances at people including myself because these people actually thought we were garbage. That is ignorant, immoral and not what Luther our king and all the humble mentors fought for in this society. We as a nation are to blame for what is happening in our world. I used to walk around thinking everyone was to blame for the way I thought and I realize I was part of the same thinking. In order for me to accept anyone, I had to accept me unconditionally. What a beautiful place to be. Now I can go anywhere anytime and I think nothing about anyone. I finally after ridding myself of all the control freaks in my life. I discovered a very elegant, graceful, and beautiful woman on my journey. The relentless pushing on me to be this way and that way was so consuming I lost who I was. Now I have one voice and that voice is trusting, loving, and the best friend I have ever had Jesus. With his patience and guidance, he has allowed me to fall but most importantly how to concentrate on myself. Every day I look deep within myself to discover what I can continue to do to become everything Jesus created me to be. I do not talk about my relationship much because that is between him and me. The one thing I learnt in life is be very careful what you say and whom you say it to. In fact, do not tell anyone anything because the realty is society is not to be trusted. Protect yourself from people do not give personal information to anyone. If you give them, something to talk about then you can count on becoming the topic of conversation. What I do for myself is my business and what I do is so good for me. Discover, Forgive and move on. We as a human race are continually looking for answers. Any answer for why the world exists. Did you ever stop to think you would never find it until you look inside of you? You have all the answers and the ones you do not have are because it is not for you to find out. We are humans the bottom of the food chain. Food has more cells in it then people do. Anyone out there that thinks they are going to find an answer to the earth and its inhabitants is crazy. Everything is in other people's viewpoint. If you want a real revelation human beings are the most unintelligent species on the planet. Animals love unconditionally but society is lost because they have not realized yet that the world is only as good as you make it and if you're looking to find answers in others good luck with that. They are just as lost as you are. In my heart, I believe that people want change they just do not know how. When you can look at yourself, see the beauty, and start to be patient and understanding to yourself then you have it. Common sense tells you that unconditional love for self is on its way. When you have fully accepted every part of yourself, feelings, looks and beliefs then you have succeeded in finding the most important Hidden Treasure in your Soul Unconditional love and acceptance. Someone who discovers this within has discovered the secret to a powerful person because nothing fazes him or her. People do not bother them, society does not bother them in fact they become free to be themselves the way god asked us to be. It is giving you permission to accept yourself. I have lived thirty some years with the idea that when I was being abused I was to accept that I deserved it. Well I have news for all you criminals and pedophiles. You have no right to do what you do. There are no excuses and yes, you deserve to be accepted, but if you think, we should accept you when you continually do crimes there is not a chance. There are millions of agencies, doctors and people in this world that would love to help you but why should I give you my precious time. LOOK INSIDE FOR ALL YOUR ANSWERS. Find out who you are and why you do this. It takes more courage to ask for help then it does to ignore the terrible wrongs you have committed. You end up hurting yourself more than anyone does and the important thing is to trust yourself, believe the decisions you make regarding your life are no one's business but yours. You do not have to tell anyone what you are doing. Society analyzes everything to death. Actually, it is not funny. Pushing their own expectations on others is the only way human beings can dump their quilt. Back off my brothers and sisters; do not look at the stick in my eye when you have a chunk of wood in yours.

CHAPTER SIX

QUIT REACTING

When I was a child, my home was so dysfunctional I was in constant reaction mode. To see human beings be controlled by one person. I watched family members tear each other apart and talk to each other with such disgust and degradation. I was always on guard I knew I was next. Respect me and listen to me what a bunch of human garbage. I became defensive, angry, degraded, and totally controlled by someone that was not even my biological family. Then I started reacting after a few years because as a child I knew I would never survive. I reacted and it was not nice. The absolute hatred I had for this family had grown to a fight back mode. I had physical fights with my siblings, I smashed my mother in the face, and it felt wonderful. Every rule and every expectation they had on me I made sure I never did. Why you ask, the reason was as a young child with my real parents and this behaviour was the scariest and most unloving place in the world. I knew in my little six year old heart that they society placed me in a home because they had money and were catholic. My own children would say get over it mom move on and because I did not do what they and everyone else wanted me to do. I charged the adoptive parents because I wanted them out of my life they were sick and never ever reached out for help for themselves which meant they thought they did nothing wrong. I do not care what any of them think. My children walked away with themselves their children and families and deserted me. Then it came to me I will never react to what my children did. In fact, the sad thing is it shows just how sick they really are. Anyone that walks away from their mother the way they did obviously has no respect for themselves or others so reacting to all the garbage is not for me. I wish the best for everyone but most of all I thank them for the peace I finally have and the respect I have for myself. I would never in my life, hurt anyone on purpose. The most disgusting hurt is the uneducated and ill-informed people they were about my illness. The reason I share this with you is to help people understand not to react when people or family do these things. The way they think and believe is none of our business everyone chooses to live by their own standards and who are we to stand in their way. It is their lives just as it is our choice whether they choose to ignore their behaviour or change it is totally up to them. From the earliest of centuries, we as a world have reacted. We have reacted with war and we have reacted with idea of slaughtering certain cultures by trying to rid the world of Jews or Ukrainians. Absolutely everywhere you go someone is reacting to something. Here is a question have you ever wondered why. I for myself have looked at my past and realized who cares, the past is done, the future is not here, yet so why focus on something you cannot change. When any human being is in an environment that is not safe, or does not feel right, we as humans react. To say human beings trust each other is a lie we do not. I cannot take a walk anymore by myself anymore and I have to watch what I say or do because this world will take whatever negative thing about you and tear you to shreds. Their reaction could be out of their own fears, anxiety, or stress. How many times do you see people walking around being cranky towards others for no good reason? They could have had a fight with their husband or they could have lost a loved one. No one knows why he or she is the way they are. Guess what stop reacting to them, which is what society wants. Society loves a reaction then they get to dump all their garbage on you. Most everyone will always take the blame. What did I do is the first question. You did not do anything it is their problem to deal with walk away. In my lifetime, I have been ridiculed, made fun of, stigmatized, demoralized and today I have no reaction to anything anymore. I also think age has so much to do with it as you get older your priorities change and being peaceful is my exercise daily. How dare anyone say anything rude or disgusting to myself or anyone around me that I care about? I have no issues standing face to face with you and telling you to walk away. We all as human beings have the same feelings and it is time to see people for who they are. When you react to someone's feelings, you are really reacting to their behaviour. Their behaviour is telling you something is wrong inside the person and it has nothing to do with you. The world is not paying any attention to you they are too engulfed with their own issues and lives. People care because they have a cozy office and a certificate that says they are trained and paid to care. My goodness, I have never been trained to care my real mother and father showed goodness because that was who they were big difference. The artificial life that we all exist in is analysed to death and because of that, we as humans react to everything. We all have to be right and we all are to live rich with a good job and go to church. Ever since I was a child, I have gone to church even when the children were younger. The realty I have never saw such a bunch of hypocrites in my life. Monday thru Friday, you can sin away and Sunday ask for forgiveness and start over. Everyone checks each other out what are you wearing and what is happening in your life. I remembering going to the church for help for my group circle of friends' people with mental illness. They refused to help me because there was no one to open the door. Then there was my dear principal such a devout catholic she played the organ at church and everyone put her in the highest of order. When the police talked to her about me she lied about everything and said she could not remember, yet I had talked to her two years before that to thank her. How convenient and so Christian of her to be honest and helpful but she was to worry that she had to live in the same town so she did what she thought was right. I never reacted, I picked up the phone and thanked her for everything and said you call yourself Christian. Everyone has taken the idea of god and turned it in to a selfish understanding and motive. God said believe in me he did not say go out there and put titles and names on churches and call them your own to reign. Jesus was human and he asks for nothing but faith. However, you as humans think you know how god wants the world to be. Jesus is within us not on the outside. As a human being, I have such a hard time with all people who gather in a building and so to speak praise the lord. Can you not do that at home in communities, families and friends. Why the spectacle, he is not asking for a show, he wants a personal relationship with you not in a crowd of people. Who is it that goes to church for recognition are you going so that they can show Joe blow that you believe in god more than others do. How ridiculous people and their motives are for credibility as a person. That does not come from any material belonging in this entire world it comes from god people. Do you truly believe that you the person should get recognition for what you have done to humanity I do not think so? If you take the time to look around you, you will see all the decisions you have made as Christians or none Christians you are sadly lead by your own ego. If you use all the tools in this book, you will come to hopefully the conclusion that humans believe they control the world and for the most part, we do. However, the real answer is, no humans do not have the capacity to take care of this world, because they are selfish, domineering and control freaks. That is not what life here is about. As a leader, you must have compassion, forgiveness, and unconditional love for all humankind. Not just the ones you arrogant people think are good enough to talk to. I have a wakeup call for all those arrogant people. I personally am tired of you and I have learnt to ignore you. Someday really soon the human race will come to and realize people like you will not be the majority. There is only one leader in this entire world and that is Jesus Christ our Saviour. The relationship you have is personal and no one has to share their beliefs to anyone it is none of their business. If you live a life of compassion and forgiveness, you do not have to say a word. Faith is the sparkle in my eye and the smile on my face. We are not on earth to answer to leaders or people that are slowly destroying our world. In fact the less information we give and the more comfort and understanding we give society will eventually understand to quit reacting to everything. I do not watch much TV just sports and I do not read the newspaper or read all the celebrity garbage. Do what you want to do but do not expect everyone to follow you. Everyone's concept of what life is to him or she is different. The talents and gifts people have are unbelievable, but the question is what are you using your gift for. Reacting to others takes away from whom you are, and what you believe in, do not give for free your important time and WALK away with no comments just a beautiful compliment how hard is that. I cannot count the number of times people around me get pissed off with me when I do not agree with them. I feel so sad for them. Why in the world does life have to be so complicated? The willingness to look at yourself and not others will open doors in the world to people and places that you never imagined. You finally have what Jesus wants for everyone freedom to be without judgement. I watched a program where people were trying to find evidence that god did not exist would you please leave god and Jesus alone. Who cares what you think let us think what we want. Quit trying to destroy and become a person who thinks he has the answers there are no answers in people. Leave the world alone; spend quality time finding ways to prosper our earth. It is time to act, not to react, take a deep breath and it is okay for you to acknowledge you do not have all the answers. You are not supposed to Jesus is doing quite fine without the ego. We are his people not yours whoever you are out there that wants to continually try to control us into believing that the only way to be happy is to be rich and famous. That is a great big lie and to tell you the truth if someday you lost everything from a tornado or earthquake people would be devastated and lost. To stop and think about the fact your still alive would mean more to me than anything. In fact, I have found within myself the need for nothing and the more I want nothing the more blessings I receive. I am the luckiest women the peace and tranquility in my life today I would never trade anyone not a penny. I found the Hidden Treasures in my Soul that have made me totally one with myself and god that is more valuable than any money or material object can ever give me. No one or thing in this life bothers me anymore. Wow it amazes me, while writing just how far I have come in my journey and the true confidence I have found and the love for me is unbelievable. In all my years of hurt, I never thought for one moment I would ever be this ecstatic about life and living yahoo. The energy I would use to react to people was terrible. I remember talking to my daughter and with all the fear of rejection, I had inside I still took the courage to beg her not to leave me. You are all that I have left and I was devastated. The rejection was shocking to me. There is nothing in the world that I have ever done to my children but raise them as best I could as a single mom. I hung up the phone and said to myself you are right my dear daughter if you as a person can do that to your own mother than yes I am walking away. With her help, she made me realize what a cold, manipulative, and cruel person she had become. Listening to her reply, I cannot talk to you anymore you make me feel bad. My answer in my head went everyone has some difficulty with the choices made in life and because she had issues, she did what she usually does and tried blame me for the denial she lives in. She has sadly a lot of heartache and I am the one she blames walk away. I care deeply for my children and they have always had the freedom to bloom. However, when someone is that hurtful to someone that gave him my son and her my daughter life. I never want to be around when karma hits and it will. People like that, are hurting, and when we learn not to react to issues like that, it gives back to the person their own garbage. We are responsible for ourselves first and foremost it is not until you fix you that you will be able to handle the world. There is no excuse in life for bad behaviour or disrespect and kids think their parents cannot walk away. They can in the end they have become adults and everyone has to answer here on earth to what they have done to those around them. We reacted when we were born it was our first cry and then we were comforted. What happen after that? There are millions and millions of self-help books out there, I know I read them. With all that information out there what excuse does humanity have for being so unkind. What in this world is so bad that we have to send our loved ones out to fight another war? Will this country ever learn from its mistakes? I do know that reaction is an instinct so it is part of who we are. I also know it is how you react that is the answer. People want to get up and fight right now. Driving down the street or just walking down the street. Some people look for trouble on purpose, that is when you walk away with your mouth shut nothing you say to that person will change the behaviour, and he or she can carry their own garbage. Reality people it is just reality. Through my life as a child, teenager, and adult the people that were to love would say horrible things to me. Most importantly, they would make sure daily I was aware how SICK I was. The truth I was a beautiful blonde curly haired little girl who had so much love for everyone. My spirit was always happy and care free. When grown men did what they did to me it made me know how sick they were. Women around me that were supposed to be mothers and wives took religion and other influences for an excuse to have no sex with their husbands along with the other cruel ideas in their sick heads. My parents were without a lie unbelievably good beautiful. The parents who adopted me, told me in many different ways how stupid they thought I was. Little did they realize I was in contact with my parent's long time before they found out? My biological mother and father along with some family members were fully aware of what this family was doing. However, because the parents who adopted me were so sick they never realized I had all the support I needed and it would only be time I would grow up. When I did I never once felt remorse for anything I did to anyone even my children. I was violent, angry and I kicked and fought them all. Now that I have given them all their responsibility back, I really could care less about anything regarding them. When people act like savages that are sick they get exactly what they deserve. I got what I deserve I am back to where I always should have been with my mother and family. Those whom participated in destroying my family and tried destroying me they are not laughing anymore and the results have just begun. They have a whole life ahead of them.

CHAPTER SEVEN

POSITIVE REINFORCEMENT

W hat has helped you get where you are today. On the other hand, are you in a situation where you have done nothing with your life and cannot understand what went wrong? Positive reinforcement is supposed to start at birth. As we learn to becoming members of our society. However, everyone thinks that just how you thought while guiding our children things happen. It is life and the first thing we seem to be teaching is right and wrong. There is no right or wrong unless you are killing people. My point is when a child is doing something that that you think is dangerous or unsafe you don't tell them no and make them feel like they did something wrong. Could we not of taken their attention away without making the child feel bad. They did nothing wrong. We are guides in this life, not human examiners. We have books telling us what to do; we have television shows telling us what to do. We came into this world as innocent children and every one of us has done our part to make sure that our actions are never admitted. Positive reinforcement leaves open the communication for people. We have the ability to discuss without looking to take confidence from any human being. Having someone reinforce what a wonderful person you are makes anyone feel good. The result is amazing. Common sense tells you if you treat people with positive reinforcement, you will indeed receive a more productive and excited person. Willing to learn whatever they want. Life becomes their own little world of achievements. Thank God, our youth got sick of how the generations have taken care of their world and now they are changing the world to a place of clean environment respect for those less fortunate. They are smarter and much more intelligent they have had enough of the garbage we gave them. Society groups the youth together and continues to label all youth as in grades. Quit teaching what is wrong and start teaching what is right about them. They are the future; I for one have more hope in them than us. Yes, I believe the youth can change this world. The strangest thing I was adopted in a home and I to this day cannot believe the negative influences that were among this family. How anyone can live with such negative dysfunctional habits and thinking is truly confusing. What else do you think comes from that kind of world? It is not wrong it is just not for me. As a child, I was given such reinforcement from my real mom and dad and their family there was never an issue for me. This was not the way to be treated and I waited until I was old enough and I got rid of them. I now have a life of positive reinforcement every day. I am treated with disrespect and my work is amazing writing books, teaching life skills. Bringing positive reinforcement to others lives is beautiful and productive. Positive Reinforcement gives you the confidence within yourself to be able to do anything in this life with no fear. It opens doors where you did not know there was one. You meet so many interesting people. You are exactly where you should be proud of yourself and what others think just does not matter anymore. There are people out there that believe they know what is good for the world. They took it upon themselves to take charge. Look where we are now. All the money in the world will not get us out of this mess. The positive reinforcement taught has brought those people around the world trying to fix the disasters made by man. If we had been given the opportunity to speak out we would have noticed how we have ignored the importance of leaving a world to be proud of. Instead, we have truth fighters now that grab attention to those who are continuously destroying our country. After all this time, we have not yet learnt patience and living simple. Simplicity makes everyone happy in the end. Our world was not created so men can figure out in the world what they can do to leave their history behind. We are all here to make life not only liveable for ourselves but for the rest of the world to enjoy. Selfish attitudes and control is not managing with positive reinforcement. We and many countries around the world are now desperate to find themselves. Their role in life is to make life better. To do that they fight and kill hundreds of innocent people because one person thinks they have the answers. Why did you people not listen? Why are you continually taking the beauty that exists all around us and making it your own. Freedom of thoughts, feelings, and expression are good for everyone. I know no one ever asked me in the years away from my own mother and father if I was happy. No one cared. Nevertheless, my family taught me the greatest gift in life and that was to respect. I did respect. Whatever this family did to me never mattered, they were and never will be someone I call my family. There negative attitudes brought nothing but the worst out in everyone. Why would anyone respect that? Respect in this life starts with yourself. My real family never gave me any reason to feel anything but proud of whom I was. I was never going to give my adoptive family something they clearly did not deserve. I survived because of the tenderness, loving kindness, and the positive affirmation from my mother and father every day. For the three or four years, I was with them they taught me how wonderful a human being I was and no one even my sisters who did not know me. How sad that things like that happen. It is important to have positive reinforcement around you at all times. No one should blame himself or herself for anything. We have today examples of negative and non-trustworthy people all around us. Our government, Churches, Schools and the list goes on. These are the fundamental resources for all people. Education cuts our Hospitals and Medicare a mess. Then there is our government. Makes me all fuzzy and warm to think we elected someone who has fraud the government for his own selfish reasons. We have more churches in the world than we do homes or shelters for those who have nothing. People gathering each Sunday to look at what people are wearing and then listening to the gossip of the week. Then we have our group called hypocrites. Jesus died on the cross after being tortured so we could have forgiveness for our sins. I do not know what others think but I truly believe he did not sacrifice his life so you can tell lies, steal, cheat, gossip, and judge through the week. Sunday because you went to church it is a new week. People actually believe because they go to church they have more moral rights then the others. Excuse me, have you lost your mind. Our churches especially the Catholics are the richest. What are we as delusional people going to do when an earthquake comes and destroys everything we have in our country? Jesus never walked with thousands he walked with few. Everything possibility in life is a reaction, from either what was taught to us or what you believe. Why does everything you do have to be a spectacle of yourself. It takes more than one person to run a country it takes people. Get out of church go home and pray so we can start using the money for all these temples and give the money to the poor starving countries. They deserve a life just like us get over yourself people it is not about you it is about the world. The passion that I share is my passion I have for life. We all deserve the best not just the few. The things you see happening in our world, dust storms, flooding, earthquakes, and this dear people is are wake up call. You have the freedom to see it how you want. We have allowed families to fight each other. We have no respect for human life or anyone around us. Have you asked yourself just how far this is going? I am personally sick of sticking my head in the sand. I will do whatever possible to bring love to someone's life that is far more expensive then that fancy house and car. No, I have hated money all my life I lived with people that said they had money and they would destroy any human being for money. Money is sick, greedy, and so manipulative. It is time to see things in the real world. Get your head out of the sand and start taking the responsibility of this life of yours? Why should the few have to take on the job themselves? Wake up and smell the coffee. One day we could wake up and have nothing but the shirt on your back and you will so wish you knew how to survive. The greedy will have nothing. All you people that think your rich realize that our government will eventually find a way to take it from you they already have. Higher ups are slowly but surely losing control and they are scared. They should be in the end we will all be the same and I cannot wait to see the How you like me now look. The answer, I do not like you and I wish you the best you are on your own. A person so hates clichés but the truth is they are tools to use that you can give yourself a reality check. Ignoring it does not make it go away not in this life. Have we not learnt enough from the mistakes in the present? Look at all the oil companies. The richest companies in the world do not care about our world. I am not scared of anyone, this is my world and my children's and grandchildren's world and you are not taking from them the opportunity for a good life not in my time. The control you all think you have is in your own mind. You will eventually be accountable for your actions. There is only one survivor, which is the one who changes their perception regarding life. We have no power. Men and Women enjoy what you can today. For life has a way of slapping you in the face. When it happens, it will happen so fast you will be devastated. If you think as a people that you will win the fight over what is happening, I am here to tell you, you will never win. The world and Mother Nature will excuse my language kick you in the ass when you least expect. If I were you, do not laugh put this in your head for a while and see how it will sit with your everyday always looking over your shoulder. It is absolutely no one's fault but your own. How about that taking responsibility, you can run and run forever but you will never be able to hide. I know that I may sound harsh but to all concerned, if we do start, listening, life will continually be an uphill battle in a world of destruction. The importance of putting positive reinforcement in our lives is here. If you stop and think about the way generations tried handling life, we all have the same memories of being ridiculed and embarrassed. People sadly found hitting or slapping was there answer to discipline. How is that positive reinforcement? I can see now that our youth and many others in teaching positions have finally realized that positive reinforcement is the answer. Slowly but surely that type of discipline is becoming less and we have finally succeeded in helping people see that there are much more constructive ways to communicate through kindness. The energy we take to be mean and less understanding is energy wasted. Positive reinforcement is what you give yourself every day. It starts with you, what you say to yourself everyday is a reflection of what you give out to the world. We are all products of our environment. It does not start at home we are in school the majority of our young years so the influences come from our teachers or other youngsters. We all learn life on the backfield at recess. It is our job as parents to become the most influential person in our child's life. As a country, we have depended on all the available people, agencies and other influences to become the one thing we aspire to. Bring back positive reinforcement in your life, at work, entertaining, or just sharing with your communities. It is our job to be the best example for everyone and that is a leader. Leaders watch out for everyone not themselves. Take a good look at your reinforcement does it need some help do not worry just give it positive reinforcement.

CHAPTER EIGHT

ENJOYING THE MOMENTS

Have you ever stopped to wonder how you are doing? Yes you, when we look back and see the changes we have made in our lives. It helps us to see just how are development is going within ourselves. I sometimes blink my eyes and realize how fast life has gone. We have the ability to look and see if the changes are positive or negative not wrong or right. Life is to be enjoyed every single day of our lives. When I was younger, I hated getting up to the day. My environment was not a pleasant one so I never enjoyed anything. Therefore, when I finally removed myself from the negative and I actually had time to breath. I realized how blessed I had become. The pace of life was the pace of others, the thoughts and my outlook was influenced by others opinion. I saw that I never really had time to enjoy my children as I had dreamed. The opportunity was gone. However, the good thing is I still have the opportunity to enjoy everything in my life now. I never ever felt like a girl. I was doing hard work with men all my life. Now I have a love for butterflies and I love bright beautiful colours, clothes and in my environment. My love of music and playing instruments is shared with all my family. My creativity I have blossomed like never before. The continued changes come from the everyday to stop and smell, taste and enjoy the little things of this life. I was very lucky, my life has taught me how to appreciate and understand human behaviour in ways that too few people would be able to understand. When you have nothing in life and you are to survive on your own, it makes life even more beautiful when it changes to the good. When I found my mother there was such a sense of relief and my mother would always say to anyone that had an opinion about me just let her be herself. After so many years, my mother comforted me with love and understanding by few words. She knows exactly what to say to me to make me feel loved. There is nothing material or human that ever brings me happiness. My love for life is the landscape and the seas and all the beautiful flowers and animals that decorate our land. There is no one in the world who appreciates people more than me. I watched many times children; mothers, sisters, and friends tear each other apart over the most undesirable things in life. Money. When you focus your attention on things that are not of the heart than you will receive what you wanted. It will continually bring anger and sorrow into your life. Your way of thinking is if I have a huge home and new vehicle and all the toys to keep us busy we will be okay. How ridiculous that is and how does that house love you. Does the car talk and tell you it loves you come on people. Stop, look, and listen. There are birds to watch, butterflies, trees, people and numerous different things to grab your attention. The moments are the time or seconds you have with your children. Listen to the stories our parents and grandparents share how enjoyable to see the difference in generations. Be excited for someone else besides yourselves. Help hold doors open for the women it does not matter how old they are. They are women and deserve to be treated with dignity and respect all the time. Women what is up with the foul language and not a woman in my lifetime will ever get along with other women. Rude, condescending and they will stop at nothing to group up and act like loud hyenas. Have you ever stopped to think about working together? Guess what, there are many women that are better looking smarter and beautiful. I see them all the time and it gives me great pleasure to tell them they are beautiful. We are all beautiful. The jealousy and negative actions regarding woman now a days is devastating. If anyone has to hurt, someone to get to what he or she thinks is the top. Then you know perfectly well you do not belong there. Time has a way of catching up to us you can lie to yourself and life is smart enough to hang around long enough to teach you the proper way to behave. I never did travel in my life it was a dream of mine to see something different in Canada. Last year opportunity showed itself and I had the most wonderful trip in a place I only read in storybooks. I felt so privileged to be a part of the world I never knew about. You know I sit here as I am writing and I am so laughing. We have in this world thousands of opportunities to do well and people think if you are angry or threatening people will leave you alone. In fact, the truth is you can stand on your head or maybe drink yourself to death the reality is. Give it a week and I am so sorry to inform you not all, but most people just carry on. I think death is beautiful I look forward to whatever lies ahead. Therefore, it does not matter what you think about how great you are. You are nothing but human and you are here for a temporary moment. In the real sense of the word, no one cares to long about anyone. There are those who will call me a big mouth bitch and hate the fact I am disturbing the pot. I just want to thank you all for taking the time to inform me of your opinion and personally could care less what you think or say. It is your business how you receive information. Oh and good luck with the attitude you get exactly what you give. By writing this, I have given no one any excuses to be anything in life but a contributing member of society. There are no excuses.

My special moments:

- 17 years old and I gave birth to my first child a baby boy-9lbs-14 ounces. I remember looking into his eyes and finding myself facing something, I never saw before a love that became bigger than I was. I would never let my children ever be hurt or abused by anyone. I would die first.
- 21 years old, I gave birth to my baby girl 3lbs-7oz. She was so beautiful and so precious.
- She was mine, and no one, even when they thought they could. Took the love I had for her. I Realized when you take what is not yours God will only allow it for so long and Mother Nature claims it and will deal with you eventually. It does not work. She was my princess and my son my prince and I will always love them.

- I found my mother and father and together we lived as family for over 20 years. My father passed away and my mother and I continue our journey.
- Writing my first book was a great challenge even when others tried to destroy it. Foolish people that believe they are superior.
- Meeting a wonderful, kind, loving, and humble man that now is my partner for life. He has never raised a voice or hand and everyday finds something small and beautiful to bring home to me for no other reason except for the fact he is proud and honoured to be part of my life. Unconditional love and acceptance something you cannot teach. I have never asked to do anything in my life with him. We accept everything about each other and everyday is a day to show each other just how much we love and respect each other.
- Most importantly, I found a friend at five years old when it was a life or death situation.
- In addition, adopted to a family only fit for animals. My friend helped me to breathe in life. He filled my heart with hope, and my soul he filled with love. He was my protection from any harm and in times of trouble.

After a long four years, I was mis-diagnosed. I am not Bi-Polar or Mentally Ill. The specialists informed me of the huge difference between my doctor's diagnoses, and the trauma I experienced. Kicked in the head by a horse and falling from the roof of a building was not Mental Illness. Nor were the continued Abuses I endured from the age of five. This to me is still a miracle I had no idea and that is okay. Total love and acceptance for who I am and who I will become in the future and I will always have the child in me to keep me humble. I have given up everything in my life to only be blessed with everything. I have a past and I have learnt I live one day at a time and sometimes moments at a time. I am so excited for tomorrow because I expect nothing and surprises come daily. You think your rich and I know I am rich in spirit, body, mind, and soul. Yes, I thought I knew what happiness was. Not a chance there is no way I could describe the feeling. All you have to do is look at my face. No wrinkles and no stress, no anxiety and free to be me. I am turning Fifty this year and when I look at myself, I see a twenty five year old.

Amazing as it seems I did not get older. I am looking younger and all I can say is thank you. I wish everyone from every lifestyle all the prayers, hope, and faith. This is your life and you are important and okay just the way you are. Live life and enjoy all of your moments as much as you can and as often as you can. This world is not going to change by itself. Instead of living an attitude of you thinking, you deserve anything. I hope that every soul looks and finally sees that this world needs us. Our world is crying for help. Do you not think it is time to think about giving back to the world what we already took for granted? We as greedy, money hungry and artificial people will end up continually taking from this world all the things that do not belong to them. Happiness, security, food on the table and a roof over your head is the only thing that is yours.

The world belongs to all of us and there is not a Government, Leader, or Power freak that needs or deserves anything in this life. You already have the greatest thing and that would be LIFE.

Get over yourselves and help fix all the devastation throughout our world. We owe it to ourselves, and all the people who are dying in this life because no one gave them the opportunity to find love. I have no idea who it was that thought life was free. Wake up call; you have to work at being human. Good luck to all and thank you for braving the opportunity to see there are so many beautiful things about his life to enjoy. Who knows I may have helped and I may not have. At least you took the first step to a life of **Personal Success**.